D0497522

GATES & FIELDS

JENNIFER FIRESTONE

ISBN: 978-0-9885399-6-9

Cover artwork by Simone Kearney
Cover, interior design, and typesetting by HR Hegnauer

Belladonna* is a reading and publication series that promotes the work of women writers who are adventurous, experimental, politically involved, multiform, multi-cultural, multi-gendered, impossible to define, delicious to talk about, unpredictable, & dangerous with language. Belladonna* is supported by funds granted by the New York State Council on the Arts, the Leslie Scalapino — O Books Fund, the Poets for the Planet Fund, the Leaves of Grass Foundation, the New York City Department of Cultural Affairs, and by generous donations from individuals. This project is made possible in part by an award from the National Endowment for the Arts. The book is also supported with a grant from the Community of Literary Magazines and Presses and the Jerome Foundation.

Library of Congress Cataloging-in-Publication Data:
    Names: Firestone, Jennifer, author.
    Title: Gates & fields / Jennifer Firestone.
    Other titles: Gates and fields
    Description: First edition. | Brooklyn, N.Y. : Belladonna Collaborative, 2017.
    Identifiers: LCCN 2016052675 | ISBN 9780988539969 (pbk. : alk. paper)
    Classification: LCC PS3606.I73 G38 2017 | DDC 813/.6--dc23
    LC record available at https://lccn.loc.gov/2016052675

Distributed to the trade by
Small Press Distribution
1341 Seventh Street
Berkeley, CA 94710
www.SPDBooks.org

Also available directly through
Belladonna*
925 Bergen Street, Suite 405
Brooklyn, NY 11238
www.BelladonnaSeries.org

 * deadly nightshade, a cardiac and respiratory stimulant, having purplish-red flowers and black berries.

Theresa Vivian Firestone

1911-2006

Albert Alan Fleischer

1919-2006

Dorothy Sarah Morrill

1944-2008

Irene Fleischer

1918-2009

CONTENTS

The Carriage held but just Ourselves —

They are telling her it's time to go
The carriage set upon the snow
To go to go they wail so the white snow
Falls onto the white snow
The lantern dims
The wheels the window the light of the eye
The horse the carriage the lantern alit
Goodbye—they are leaving

GATES

Where's the gate door

Take flowers home

Adornment dies immediately

The language on the stone

Shapes are shapes

These are all rectangular

A gate behind a gate

Would some say grates or iron vines?

Is this to own or to think of as home?

Is there a gate-keeper?

What is the meadow of this space?

Beyond the gates
The wrought iron's lace
Hands through iron pockets

A boned instrument
scaling the gate
A jackrabbit's playing
and pleasured
by its hopping
The sour grass
lime wet

This place previously in a vision   Wet pen drawn at the line

A place religiously tied   religiously religiously

A person, place or thing

Bring thy pebble or thy flowers or thy inscription
Bring bring bringeth your love
Dear ones bringeth your love

Ashes to trees

The trees!

This place a concrete place
A place to be bought and sold
A place or stationary object
First come words then memories
Then parting words
The trees! *shhh* The trees!
A whistling has begun *shhh*
A whistling has begun
Here and beyond here
Here and beyond

There was once paper   Now paper floats

Now flaps

The crumpled form addresses stone

The wood cracks its bone in the distance

The forms see no other forms

Webs shine in early light

The long tree's bristle

A hermetic cry

Will attentions be unified?

Can they together this?

A vase of dust
Stone wisps
Tiny species
A vase of dust
Fog evaporating
A night call
Grass

A vase's ancient imprints
Trees
Lines
Singing
Blot

A vase of dust
Lines
Song
Sings

FIELDS

The field this way and that, the field arising
The field footholds, the field of an eye and mind
The sky, the field startlingly aware
Sky, observing field containing nothing
The sky's eye, field shockingly aware
The field this way the field that

In a field
with or without wilderness
with or without universal skies
with or without a written stage
with or without an animal with leaves
there may be a miraculous shower

If present
hot still silence abides
hot space without stifling
hot space with a center cool
presently unafraid of this

A lineless horizon with no individual markings

There is no safety but a mind is safe
                    Safely thrown across the field

At the point of no one's land
The field contains seeds

Presently attend to this whole space   Not a designated marker
Perhaps presently attending   The field fills eyes
Perhaps peace
With what is not seen the field is busy

The field sings
Blanket of verse
Will earth quake
Mistress or unanimous
Earth hollowly
Quaking

The secret eyes of field life
The secret life of wheat gazing
The wind suns itself upon the wheat

Instruction of location rattles
Under the oak it aches
The field wells, the field waters
The field signifies the field

A faraway whistle, lightning at the edge of dirt
And where do the footsteps take you what place might you rest

SHE

To say she will face their absence
To this notion to this
Waiting for the objects to embody
Waiting for the signature to seal

She's working her way through
The fields admonish her labor

Oh why must there be expanse so beckoningly at my disposal?

The moon is another
field or is it the sun reflecting none

She's working her way through the field

Is that a star in my eye or the sky, is that a you from whom I have known?

She's sleeping in the field

She wails as she works, wails as she reads:
Absence is where the answer lies

The dream of snow, the light flooding
The dirt heaving

I do confess I lost them

Signs and symbols when the bird fell yes it did
before the feet of many
And the black air beneath her eyes came to her as writing
as a text to read
And she repeated with the echoes of scripting
She chimed two tones:

My we love please bringeth the peace that resides
My we love please watch with thine eyes to this day

And if the wheels come to a halt they will just with sound carry

She's in no quick hurry but circumstance unbeknownst
She's planting with a bare hand hacking remorse away
She's a worker in the day
With no mentioning otherwise

Why are you so close to me with the shine that is blinding?
That there is no divinity oh I say to you in waking day
I say run your carriage the other way my property unwelcoming

The hum
Birds falling
The dew's density

Cutting through   A machine will leave its wails   The animal beyond moon
The glimpse of hay or insect   Motion   Milkless   Dying

The bell didst holler she responding   *I'm not home not home*   Responding

Earth ran red to feet   Housing bodies   Earthly casing

What the cows brought   How the structures stood   How the sounds conjoined

Is it desire at thy feet sweet one, is it my own ungraciousness to turn thy blind eye
unto such a giving face

Bushels   Sweet grass   The horse broke loose late morning

The story replicating

LEAVING

Anonymous
A speck among many,
As everyday new specks become something they become nothing
They say memories and the wind blows   They say memories
and the wind blows   Can they recall its sound

An egg became   And light rose and light rose
An egg became

The light took its greatest speed the light ran and ran

The language is failing at its first birth
moments before it doesn't have a chance
it gasps for air and then fills imploding
it doesn't have a chance yet the mind requires
its running, closing the clasp over and over

Before the last look a mouth flutters open   *oh*   *oh*
When was the mind relieved
Before or after such looks of horror   The machine regulating   *I do see*   *I do*
Like the worst plot   that deathly glance
And then she too fell wisely

And like the weather say you
The timeliness of day   Chimes
Dusk to dawn to
The oldest sun returns

Or what will grow numerously
In the hostile room where white appears
Food shoots through pipes
Whitened
The moss laying bare its body

The sight of
Skin
The bones baring
He a
Gentle-man

The room contains
Feeling, how a room
Breathes
The body fixed
The mind
Unsettles

The body fixed
Unsettles
The mind
The room it
Contains

The bodies watch his body
Fold and scratch, might they say:
"Fold and scratch"

And when it flattened the word silence leaving or left the silencing
Though flattened what is seen what movement imperceptible
Spirals, escapes, distills, what we say energy, matter

They may or may not be with us
In this room, they may
Not be
We elaborate as he leaves,
Upon his devices,
His machinery, his son and his daughter
Willingly
Devised

Or she came across the land
To be in her bed-chamber before she thus retired
To hold her dangled hand
To receive her in this such
State but when arriving she had expired as such

Or by which he medicated her and telephoned her and
Attended the attendees who were but near her and
Said here are my instructions despite
And the last gripping moment he seized her eyes
To sight her drowning, sounds internally
As she waved him out the door

Or she the mouth sagged when speaking
Words slid past lips
The person operating the mouth
Aware

Moments swept and then escaped
Waiting with our breath for release
What have thy done with the death-bed?
What have we structured, what goodliness can
We bequeath from events that are but fleeting
A dostly good chamber to be a member
Because we needn't not remember
Our thinking seized

The beat of heart gone, respiration, brain, nerves

GONE

Red brayed red breaking gradient razed   red, red

Beneath the middle of it   the note   seared   plucked the growth   flying

Small cloud

Where is she   where?

Slide   whisking   slide   sheer ice of metal   opening like flesh   one   slide

Like the plates being passed   cut   in air delivered   handed over   to

A box to put her in and slide, to put her in and slide, to put her in injected
and slide to shelf contents, slide, a river doesn't belong in a dam, a river
doesn't want to be put, a she is in a drawer, slid, filed, none

They say time is an antidote   Clink   They say at least she saw the family
Clink   They say   she became open   Clink   Clink

To this they shall not drink or promise that they know the right ways
The path is not a path

Guilt and other small planets colliding

When he chose not to visit her site
When he saw her dressed in the box
When she saw the first shovel of dirt
The dead leaves bashed by
sun surmise it is already
everywhere

Afraid to touch the skin of those so close
Embracing becomes more difficult
Loss becomes tangible post-loss

To fall to that place   And then to return   so quickly
White flag snaps   The frame and its contents aware   These other
chapters long ago frayed

The mind can't be placed to these thoughts   Fluttering   Erase
When flying to the frame   Erase
The knowledge of her   instantly erasing
Speaking erase   Raise the tongue
        Erase

Because she shut like a lamp
because the receiver soon became sound
because weakness bespeaks such circumstances
because clatter and such are the mechanics
because she did and then done
because if just saying then doing is not

SHE

She bringing her hands through the field
The thistle sweeping her by
The wind or moan of field
The sheep
The mind deep into earth

She ravenously working
She carrying sacks placing them she tidying rows

As if before before she motioning through

And in yesteryears when days seemed long
A bell around her very neck
We were there saying *come what you are*
We were there saying

Held to the light that was leaving
She sees herself vanishing
She walks the miles till land is milk

And the crack of lightning on her skin the hole in the ground
The wash of water that was sweeping and rose
The signs of the book that bled:

Oh please my love my prayer my tiny ability
My words that burn to fire and then no more

She a field thrice surviving she a field unbeknown   She

Like a plague say you this rain of nothing when I shook it nothing shook

And the pheasant nearby and the bending flower

Nobody has asked who I am, nobody wants to know

And if it comes the carriage

I will you now through the space of trees allotting
Through the passage that detours its direction

CHORUS

She authenticates herself unknowingly
She has laid her vision bare
We collaborate our chorusing
She has laid her vision bare

Yes but just say it   She is just one body   Hardly there
We can say field and feel it because we did not designate
The sky turned pages and the language rained   We do not hesitate

Oh there she is a-whispering   telling of night-thoughts and murmurs
We hear a gate close and yet it's open   A home of sorts that is tidy and warm
A bell is rung   The old tree hanging   Words not needed to enjoy the warmth

To this we all shall rise   To this we have just risen

I think she has gone home
I think she is all alone
The latch is in her mind without it she feels we will escape
The latch is her mind and we escaped so long ago
Her words fail her brutally
She can sow the land so tenderly
A sun-moon lit our bodies
And we lost our shape quite naturally

The latch of this is broken the latch of this is open
The latch of this is broken the latch of this is open

She is picking flowers at the entrance, snapping tiny stems
She is thinking presently about the flowers only

We are in this time   All has been done

There is she who is here in our space so near
There is she who is here in our space so near
Her work may or may not have gone to waste
Her waste is re-defining as this night-star sun

The various shapes are we collecting down the trees
We will come from the leaves down the trees
We are more confident in this space than she
We impress ourselves this way
Our perception is the light, the light

GATES & FIELDS

The stark lines of habitat
The promise to contain
If legible on the line the plot will be granted

The footprint ne'er soiling the woman's home
as freshly planted near her stone
The gate's flowers neatly groomed
as sun magnificently shown

The quick wings that flew through the grates
to greet the wildness of brush
The different-aged trees
where the seeds dispersed

The field never occupied though occupants exist
The deer gathered in a corner and what with the sounds
The field sounds the field sounds

Might not they both be bookmarks
Might not they both hold our minds as resting place
Whether cries or prayer,
whether skeleton or ash,
A place, a location for those left behind

The gates held the family while the field flew
The gates held the hands that worked the land
The gates held the smaller stones and bigger stones
The field left to grow and over-grow so one field
was layers of field and fields and fields

SHE

Milk to the land   whitens

A horse might surely tread   A path

The wheat wet   A shadow-sun

A path might find a horse's tread

Did I not promise, rise to this?

The sun   red

The bell   escaping

I am not surely dead

The carriage halts, the morning breathes
The carriage shakingly aware

The carriage halts upon the ground, wheels stir without a sound
The carriage drives from day to night, from dawn to dawn, a burning light
The carriage gathers thoughts lifts them to the sky as birds
The sky as birds the carriage leads, the sky as birds the carriage leaves

What became one became none
again and again an eye spots an eye
again and again a sea cries to sea
Oh are you near
who might be listening
again and again place the word to the air
just there
again and again the carriage will stop
and she will listen

Rest in its deepest states
we name slumber
And the field covers her
again and again

And if you and you are here then say it   say it
I am but one and you are many
Lights in the day   ringing

And a gate might open
To a gate

Might open

AUTHOR'S NOTE

Voices—they may have been ghosts. They sang and instructed.
A woman from another time appeared. She was working in a field.
She was trying to rid herself of ghosts.
She was a ghost.

Prayers and chants spontaneously revealed.

Then a palette, patches of color, broad strokes of land—the field and
the gates, where bodies and spirits and nature might be found.

Place became corporeal.

Words scattered and landed.

Because I could not stop for death.
Because the carriage was a vehicle for grief that wouldn't move despite
life passing.

ACKNOWLEDGMENTS

Grateful acknowledgment to *Boog City*, *How2*, *Lightning'd Press*, *Pinstripe Fedora*, *Ping-Pong Literary Journal*, and *Saint Elizabeth Street*, where versions of some of these poems first appeared. With special thanks to Brenda Iijima of Portable Press at Yo-Yo Labs for publishing part of this book as the chapbook *Waves*, and to Brenda Hillman for awarding *Gates & Fields* the 2014 Marsh Hawk Press Robert Creeley Memorial Prize.

Deep thanks to Belladonna* Collaborative, particularly Emily Skillings and Marcella Durand, and also to Krystal Languell, Rachel Levitsky, and HR Hegnauer for their attentiveness and insights. Much thanks to Kazim Ali, CAConrad, Susan Howe, Dana Teen Lomax, Jill Magi, Eileen Myles, Sarah Rosenthal, Laura Sims, Joanna Sondheim, Cole Swensen, Anne Waldman, and Leni Zumas. Thanks to Lynne and Fred Firestone, and always to Jonathan Morrill, Ava, Judah, and Iris, for their love and support.

ABOUT THE AUTHOR

Jennifer Firestone was raised in San Francisco and now lives in Brooklyn. She is an Assistant Professor of Literary Studies at Eugene Lang College (The New School). Her books include *Swimming Pool* (DoubleCross Press), *Flashes* (Shearsman Books), *Holiday* (Shearsman Books), *Waves* (Portable Press at Yo-Yo Labs), *from Flashes* (Sona Books), *snapshot* (Sona Books), and *Fanimaly* (Dusie Kollektiv). Firestone co-edited (with Dana Teen Lomax) *Letters To Poets: Conversations about Poetics, Politics and Community* (Saturnalia Books). Firestone has work anthologized in *Kindergarde: Avant-Garde Poems, Plays, Songs, & Stories for Children* and *Building is a Process / Light is an Element: essays and excursions for Myung Mi Kim.* Firestone won the 2014 Marsh Hawk Press Robert Creeley Memorial Prize.